CORNERSTONES
OF FREEDOM™

THE HUNT FOR BIN LADEN

BY JOSH GREGORY

CHILDREN'S PRESS®
An Imprint of Scholastic Inc.
New York   Toronto   London   Auckland   Sydney
Mexico City   New Delhi   Hong Kong
Danbury, Connecticut

BRINGING
HISTORY
to LIFE

Content Consultant
James Marten, PhD
Professor and Chair, History Department
Marquette University
Milwaukee, Wisconsin

Library of Congress Cataloging-in-Publication Data
Gregory, Josh.
 The hunt for Bin Laden / by Josh Gregory.
 pages cm.—(Cornerstones of freedom)
 Includes bibliographical references and index.
 Audience: Ages 9–12.
 Audience: Grades 4–6.
 ISBN 978-0-531-28209-0 (lib. bdg.) — ISBN 978-0-531-27674-7 (pbk.)
 1. Bin Laden, Osama, 1957–2011—Juvenile literature. 2. War on Terrorism,
2001–2009—Juvenile literature. 3. Terrorism—United States—Juvenile literature. 4. United States. Navy. SEALs—History—21st century—Juvenile
literature. 5. Qaida (Organization)—Juvenile literature. 6. Afghan War,
2001– —Juvenile literature. I. Title.
 HV6432.G747 2013
 363.325'160973—dc23   2013001358

All rights reserved. Published in 2014 by Children's Press, an imprint of
Scholastic Inc.
Printed in the United States of America 113

SCHOLASTIC, CHILDREN'S PRESS, CORNERSTONES OF FREEDOM™,
and associated logos are trademarks and/or registered trademarks of
Scholastic Inc.

1 2 3 4 5 6 7 8 9 10 R 23 22 21 20 19 18 17 16 15 14

Photographs © 2014: Alamy Images: 25 (Ton Koene), 36 (US Navy Photo);
AP Images: 2, 3, 10, 11, 57 top, 58 (Al-Jazeera), 28 (Aqeel Ahmed), 6
(Chao Soi Cheong), 33 (Charles Dharapak), 18 (David Guttenfelder), 29
(DigitalGlobe), 34 (J. Scott Applewhite), 22 (Jim Bourg), 14 (John Gaps III),
4 bottom, 43 (Justin Sullivan/Getty Images), 40 (Manuel Balce Ceneta), 12,
55 (Mark Lennihan), 46 (Maya Alleruzzo), 8 (Portland Police Department),
5 top, 35, 45 (Rex Features), 5 bottom, 20 (Scott Nelson), 42 (Susan
Walsh), 19 (U.S. Air Force, Staff Sgt. Jeremy T. Lock), 16, 56 bottom (Win
McNamee), 4 top, 15 (Zaheeruddin Abdullah), 13; Media Bakery: cover;
Reuters/Parwiz Parwiz: 39; REX USA: 30; Shutterstock, Inc.: 24, 56 top
(Albert H. Teich), 49, 59 (Carolina K. Smith MD); Superstock, Inc./Photri
Images: 7; U.S. Department of Defense/MSgt Cecilio Ricardo: 23, 57 bot-
tom; U.S. Navy: 51 (Photographer's Mate 3rd Class Dusty Howell), 32; US
Air Force/Lt. Col. Leslie Pratt: 26; White House Photo/Pete Souza: back
cover, 48, 54; XNR Productions, Inc.: 52, 53.

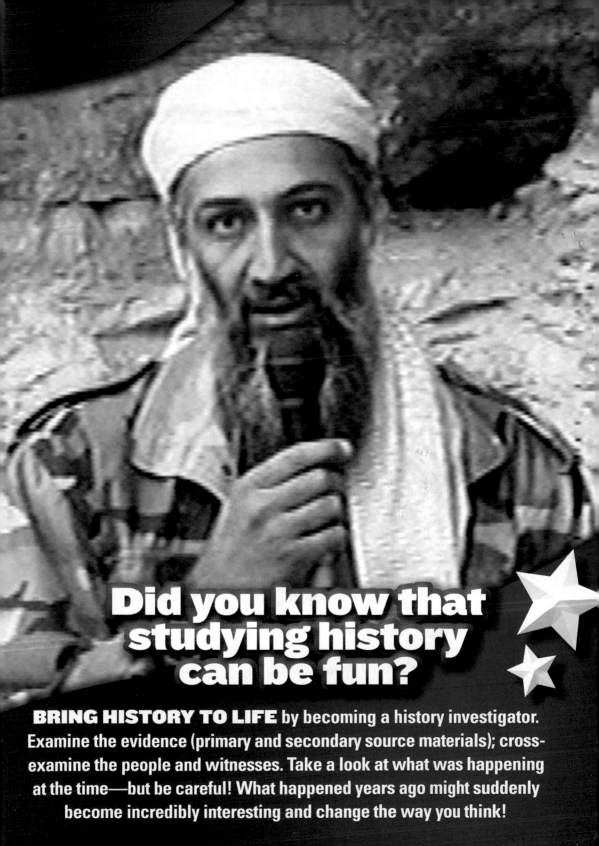

Did you know that studying history can be fun?

BRING HISTORY TO LIFE by becoming a history investigator. Examine the evidence (primary and secondary source materials); cross-examine the people and witnesses. Take a look at what was happening at the time—but be careful! What happened years ago might suddenly become incredibly interesting and change the way you think!

Contents

Day of Devastation

More than 3,000 people were killed in the horrific terrorist attacks in the United States on September 11, 2001.

On the morning of September 11, 2001, the people of the United States were shocked by a terrorist attack unlike anything they had ever witnessed. Millions across the

NINETEEN TERRORISTS TOOK PART

nation watched in horror as TV news channels reported that an airplane had crashed into the North Tower of the World Trade Center in New York City. At first, it seemed like it might have been an accident. But about 18 minutes later, a second airplane hit the South Tower.

About 40 minutes after the attack on the South Tower, a third airplane slammed into the Pentagon, a building near Washington, D.C., that is home to the U.S. Department of Defense. Then, a fourth and final plane crashed into a field in Pennsylvania about a half hour later. It had likely been on course to crash into yet another major target, but its passengers had heroically taken control of it back from the terrorists who had **hijacked** the plane. As thousands of people struggled to escape the devastated buildings in New York and Washington, the rest of the world attempted to make sense of the shocking news.

September 11, 2001, marked the 60th anniversary of the groundbreaking for the Pentagon's construction.

IN THE 9/11 AIRPLANE HIJACKINGS.

CHAPTER 1

THE HUNT BEGINS

Security camera footage revealed terrorists Mohamed Atta (right) and Abdulaziz al-Omari (left) passing through airport security in Portland, Maine, on the morning of September 11, 2001.

IN THE DAYS FOLLOWING

September 11, Americans wanted to know who was responsible for the horrific actions. Many called for the United States government to seek swift revenge against the attackers. Because all of the hijackers had died during the attacks, information was scarce at first. Details about the terrorists and their goals, however, slowly began coming to light. One of the hijackers on board the plane that crashed into the North Tower was a man named Mohamed Atta. Before boarding the plane in Boston, Massachusetts, Atta had taken another flight from Portland, Maine. During this flight, his luggage was left behind in Maine. When authorities searched the luggage, they found evidence that tied Atta to an Islamic **extremist** group called al-Qaeda.

Osama bin Laden's October 7, 2001, video message showed him inside a hidden cave surrounded by weapons.

Finding the Culprits

U.S. authorities soon announced that al-Qaeda was the main suspect in the attacks. The group, led by a man named Osama bin Laden, denied these charges at first. However, in October, bin Laden released an 18-minute video in which he claimed that al-Qaeda was directly involved in the attacks. In the video, he promised that the group would continue its assault on the United States.

Millions of grieving people finally had a villain upon whom they could focus their anger. In a few weeks, bin Laden went from being a terrorist leader generally unknown among Americans to the country's most widely hated enemy.

About one month after September 11, Osama bin Laden released a video recording in which he acknowledged al-Qaeda's responsibility for the attacks. Immediately, he became the most hated man in the United States. See page 60 for a link to view a news report that includes translated clips from bin Laden's video.

The Roots of Terror

Bin Laden was born in Riyadh, Saudi Arabia, in 1957. His father had at least 50 children from multiple wives. His father was a billionaire owner of a construction business with ties to the country's royal family. Bin Laden

Bin Laden's second-in-command, Ayman al-Zawahiri, was also shown in the October 7 video footage. Al-Zawahiri took over leadership of al-Qaeda following bin Laden's death.

YESTERDAY'S HEADLINES

In the immediate aftermath of the September 11 attacks, Americans were left angry, confused, and grief-stricken. Many news reports captured the feelings of the people who had experienced the tragedy firsthand. One woman interviewed in the *New York Times* waited for news of her boyfriend, who worked in the World Trade Center. "I don't know exactly what I should be doing. Where should I go?" she asked. Another New Yorker, in the process of fleeing Manhattan, told reporters, "It's devastating, just looking back at that scene. The smoke, the darkness. It's like the day stood still."

attended college in his home country and studied business administration. At about this time, he also began studying religion with well-known Islamic extremists.

In 1979, the Soviet Union invaded the almost entirely Muslim nation of Afghanistan. The invasion began a conflict that would be known as the Afghan War. Bin Laden and many others who shared his views saw the Soviet aggression as an attack not just on Afghanistan but also on the religion of Islam. They began planning resistance against the Soviets. Soon after the war began, bin Laden traveled to Afghanistan. There he worked with other resistance leaders to raise money and recruit soldiers to fight the Soviets.

Muslim rebels known as mujahideen fought against Soviet military intervention in Afghanistan during the Afghan War.

Building the Base

In 1988, the Afghan War was still going strong. That year, bin Laden used his vast list of resistance volunteers to build a computer database of people who were sympathetic to his cause. He used this database to establish his own loose organization of Islamic militants. He called it al-Qaeda, which means "the base" in Arabic.

The following year, the Soviets finally withdrew from Afghanistan. Bin Laden and his allies had been victorious, but they did not believe that their struggle had completely ended. With the Soviets gone, al-Qaeda began to focus on other targets that it believed to be enemies of its extreme Islamic beliefs. Sometimes this meant working to eliminate foreign influences on Muslim nations. Other times, it meant fighting against Muslim leaders who did not share the same extreme views as bin Laden.

Bin Laden and al-Qaeda viewed the United States as one of their greatest enemies. The United States had been involved in several conflicts in Muslim nations, including the Persian Gulf War of 1991. As a result, bin Laden and other extremists believed that the United States was attempting to force its values and culture on the entire Muslim world.

During the Persian Gulf War of 1991, U.S. troops helped force invading Iraqi forces out of Kuwait.

Throughout the 1990s, al-Qaeda grew and spread its influence into many different countries. In 1996, the group was forced out of its headquarters in Sudan by that country's government. Once again, bin Laden traveled to Afghanistan, where he had first made a name for himself. There al-Qaeda received the assistance of a militant group known as the Taliban. The Taliban had taken control of Afghanistan's government in the years following the Afghan War. It was known for its extremist views and support of Islamic terrorist groups.

SPOTLIGHT ON

TOYOTA

The Taliban

After Soviet forces left Afghanistan in 1989, a civil war raged as the country's people fought for control of the national government. Soon, the nation had splintered into many different sections, each controlled by different military leaders. In 1994, the Taliban (meaning "students" in Arabic) formed in Afghanistan. It began defeating these military leaders in an effort to unify the country and take control for itself. Many people, tired of war after so many years, supported the Taliban despite its extreme views. By the end of the decade, the group had gained control of almost the entire country.

Al-Qaeda continued to become stronger. Though bin Laden operated out of Afghanistan, the group had members and military training camps in many countries. It also formed relationships with other like-minded

Speaker of the House Dennis Hastert (left) and Senator Robert Byrd (right) stood behind President George W. Bush as he delivered a speech on September 20, 2001, calling for the Taliban to hand over the al-Qaeda leaders responsible for the September 11 attacks.

terrorist groups. With this power at his disposal, bin Laden began planning the September 11 attacks.

War in Afghanistan

Once the United States knew that bin Laden was responsible for the events of September 11, the government began its attempt to hunt him down. In a speech given on September 20, 2001, President George W. Bush publicly demanded of the Taliban, "Deliver to United States authorities all the leaders of al-Qaeda who hide in your land."

Taliban leader Mullah Mohammed Omar refused to give in to Bush's demands. He and the rest of the Taliban supported bin Laden and al-Qaeda. They were willing to offer al-Qaeda terrorists protection from the U.S. government. Bush and other U.S. leaders knew that to have any chance of capturing bin Laden, they would first need to end the Taliban's control in Afghanistan.

The United States secretly began preparing for war on the Taliban by sending Central **Intelligence** Agency (CIA) **operatives** to Afghanistan on September 26. The CIA team began working with anti-Taliban Afghans to make plans for toppling the Taliban leadership. Soon, U.S. and British troops arrived in the country, bringing weapons and helping to train their Afghan allies.

On October 7, U.S. and British airplanes began bombing Taliban targets. With the combined strength of these air attacks and the efforts of U.S., British, and Afghan troops on the ground, the first stage of the war went quickly. By December 6, the allied forces had taken control of Kandahar, the Taliban's home city.

Escape from Tora Bora

The Taliban was far from being completely defeated. It had been weakened enough, however, for the United States and its allies to begin searching for bin Laden. By the middle of December, they determined that he had been hiding in the mountains of northeastern Afghanistan, in a series of caves known as Tora Bora, since at least November. Bin Laden had carefully chosen his mountain hideout because he knew that it would be difficult for anyone looking for him to reach him there. Because he was in rocky mountain **terrain** and deep within a system of caves, the only way enemy troops could reach him would be on foot.

Despite the difficulty of getting to bin Laden, U.S. and British soldiers accompanied a force made up mainly of Afghan troops in an assault on Tora Bora. The Afghans were not trained professional soldiers. They were simply people who wanted to end the Taliban's rule over their country. As a result, they were not very effective against the well-trained al-Qaeda fighters. The Afghans also refused to fight at night. This allowed bin Laden's men to easily take back any ground they lost during a day's

An anti-al-Qaeda fighter is shown here patrolling Afghanistan's White Mountains, which are home to the Tora Bora cave complex.

Even though the U.S. military devoted a great deal of energy searching for Osama bin Laden, he managed to stay hidden for several years after his escape from Tora Bora.

fighting, making progress very slow for the allies. But instead of sending more support, U.S. leaders insisted on pressing forward with the men they had. This decision gave bin Laden the opportunity he needed to escape. The al-Qaeda mastermind fled across the nearby border into the country of Pakistan in December 2001.

In the following years, the war continued, but bin Laden remained safely hidden. The United States had missed its best chance at capturing the man responsible for the September 11 attacks. He could not stay hidden forever, though.

CHAPTER 2

A RENEWED EFFORT

U.S. troops are scheduled to remain in Afghanistan until at least 2014.

As the war in Afghanistan continued over the following years, finding bin Laden became a less important priority for U.S. intelligence agencies. It was not until the spring of 2008 that certain U.S. intelligence agents began focusing once more on capturing the al-Qaeda leader. Their first several plans failed to turn up any useful information. Eventually, agents decided to follow known al-Qaeda **couriers** until one of them led the agents to bin Laden.

Barack Obama (right) defeated John McCain (left) in the 2008 presidential election after a series of debates in which both candidates outlined their views on issues such as the war in Afghanistan and the hunt for Osama bin Laden.

A New Leader

As CIA agents worked to find bin Laden in Pakistan, Americans were gearing up for the 2008 presidential election. With President Bush's second term coming to an end, American voters would have to choose a new leader. During one debate between the leading contenders, Democratic candidate Barack Obama was asked what he would do if bin Laden were discovered hiding in Pakistan. Obama replied clearly: "If we have Osama bin Laden in our sights and the Pakistani government is unable, or unwilling, to take [him and these militants] out, then I think we have to act and we will take them out. We will kill bin Laden. We will crush al-Qaeda. That has to be our biggest national security policy."

A FIRSTHAND LOOK AT
THE 2008 PRESIDENTIAL DEBATES

Many experts believe that Barack Obama's strong stance against terrorism in the 2008 presidential debates helped him win the election later that year. See page 60 for a link to watch video clips of Obama speaking about the search for bin Laden.

Obama won the election in November 2008. Soon after he took office on January 20, 2009, he began working to fulfill the promise he had made during the debate. He met with recently appointed CIA director Leon Panetta to discuss the issue. "We need to redouble our efforts in hunting bin Laden down, and I want us to start putting more resources, more focus, and more urgency into that mission," Obama said. Many people in

Almost immediately after his inauguration in January 2009, President Obama initiated a renewed effort to track down Osama bin Laden.

SPOTLIGHT ON

Leon Panetta

Leon Panetta was born in Monterey, California, in 1938. After graduating from college and law school, Panetta joined the U.S. Army in 1964. He served for two years before moving to Washington, D.C., where he began his political career. After working as an assistant to a U.S. senator, he was named director of the U.S. Office of Civil Rights in 1969. In 1976, Panetta was elected to the U.S. House of Representatives, from the state of California. He served until 1993, when he left to become President Bill Clinton's chief of staff. When President Obama took office in 2009, he appointed Panetta the new director of the CIA.

the United States and around the world were still anxious to see bin Laden captured and punished. As time had passed, however, the CIA had devoted fewer and fewer resources to the effort. Obama asked Panetta to create a "detailed operation plan" for finding the hidden terrorist. He wanted to "ensure that [the government] expended every effort" in finally locating bin Laden.

The Plan Pays Off

Meanwhile, intelligence operatives overseas were continuing to keep an eye on al-Qaeda's couriers. One of the men they had targeted was named Abu Ahmed al-Kuwaiti. In the summer of 2010, operatives tracked al-Kuwaiti to the city of Peshawar, Pakistan. They soon began following his every movement.

U.S. officials did not expect to find bin Laden in a city such as Abbottabad, which is located just 5 miles (8 kilometers) from the Pakistan Military Academy and is home to many of Pakistan's military leaders.

Eventually, al-Kuwaiti led his hidden pursuers to the small city of Abbottabad in Pakistan. It was not the sort of place the operatives would have expected to find a terrorist leader in hiding. Instead, it was a prosperous city filled with vacationers and high-ranking members of the Pakistani military.

Intelligence operatives watched as al-Kuwaiti drove to a compound located on the outer edge of the city. The home was oddly well fortified, given its location in a middle-class neighborhood. The compound consisted of a three-story main building, a smaller guesthouse, and other small buildings. The buildings were enclosed by huge concrete walls that ranged between 12 and 18 feet

(3.7 and 5.5 meters) high and had barbed wire stretched along the top. There were also several fences protecting the compound, and the house's windows were blocked so no one could see inside. With such defenses, it was clear that someone was hiding inside.

Watching the Compound

The Americans did not know whether bin Laden was inside, but it was obvious that the compound was worthy of their close observation. Keeping careful **surveillance** on it at all times, however, would be an extremely challenging task. How would intelligence operatives manage to avoid alerting the compound's occupants that someone was

Drones such as the MQ-9 Reaper allow the U.S. military to observe and attack its targets from a distance, reducing the risk that its troops will be harmed.

watching them? The Americans also did not want the Pakistani government to know about the operation. They feared that if they revealed their plans to the Pakistanis, the information could leak to the people in the compound and give them a chance to escape.

Operatives used a variety of methods to secretly keep tabs on the comings and goings at the compound. Airborne **drones** and satellites took photos and videos of the compound from a distance. The operatives also spied on the compound from a nearby **safe house** that they set up. The agents used radar to look for any hidden tunnels that might be underneath the

A VIEW FROM ABROAD

Although Pakistan was an ally of the United States, many of its leaders would not necessarily be helpful in capturing bin Laden or other terrorists hiding in their country. Many Pakistani leaders believed that U.S. forces conducting **raids** in Pakistan was a violation of Pakistan's **sovereignty**.

One U.S. operation in late 2008 was meant to be a quick attack on a known al-Qaeda compound. The raid, however, turned into a blazing gun battle. About two dozen people were killed, including several **civilians**. After this incident, the Pakistani government warned the United States that unauthorized raids would not be tolerated in the future. This put U.S. intelligence operatives in a difficult position when it came to keeping watch over the mysterious compound in Abbottabad.

The Abbottabad compound was equipped with heavy defenses such as thick concrete walls, yet it was in plain sight of any visitors to the neighborhood.

compound. They even visited nearby homes to ask questions about the complex, pretending to be people who wanted to build similar houses in the neighborhood.

Despite their efforts, the operatives were unable to figure out who was living in the compound. They did, however, discover several interesting facts. The people living inside the compound were very careful not to let any clues about their identity escape the facility. Intelligence also revealed that there was no telephone or Internet access behind the compound's massive walls. Oddly, the people in the compound also burned their trash instead of leaving it out for collectors.

Taking Action

The CIA soon began using an advanced new kind of drone. It was equipped with state-of-the-art surveillance and **stealth** technology. This technology allowed the drone to take extremely detailed photos and videos from high above the compound while staying out of sight of the Pakistani government.

The new drone gave U.S. intelligence its first glimpse of a man living in the compound. Operatives carefully examined photos of the man. But because they were taken from above, his face could not be seen clearly.

The images also revealed that several other people lived in the compound with the unknown man. Several of them stayed at all times within the protective walls that surrounded the buildings, never leaving for any reason.

U.S. drones took detailed photographs of the compound and the surrounding area from high in the sky, allowing intelligence officials to search for clues that might identify the people living inside.

CHAPTER 3

PLANS AND PREPARATIONS

President Obama routinely received intelligence briefings from Leon Panetta (right) and other top advisers.

PRESIDENT OBAMA'S

intelligence advisers first told him about the compound at the end of the summer in 2010. They were careful to inform him that they did not know who was living there. They were relatively certain, however, that the compound had at least some links to al-Qaeda. They told the president that the compound was the best lead they had on bin Laden in years. Obama knew that it was important not to act too quickly. He wanted to make sure there was strong evidence that bin Laden was in the compound before ordering a raid. Yet he also knew that waiting too long could waste a rare opportunity to get the man responsible for the September 11 attacks.

William McRaven

William McRaven began his military career as a journalism student at the University of Texas, where he was a member of the Naval Reserve Officers Training Corps. After graduating, he began a long career as a naval officer and studied to become an expert in special operations. In June 2008, he began putting his expertise to use as commander of the Joint Special Operations Command (JSOC). In this position, McRaven studied the tactics, equipment, and training used for special operations in the U.S. military and found ways to improve them. He was also in charge of planning high-profile special operations in conflicts across the world.

Discussing the Options

In February 2011, Panetta met with Vice Admiral William H. McRaven. McRaven was the commander of the Joint Special Operations Command (JSOC), an organization in charge of planning special operations within the U.S. military. He had overseen many missions to capture and kill terrorist leaders and other enemies of the United States. Panetta and McRaven agreed that any potential raid on the compound would require cooperation between JSOC and the CIA.

On March 14, 2010, Obama held a meeting at the White House to discuss potential options for conducting a raid on the compound. Several ideas were proposed. Each had positive and negative aspects. Conducting an air strike on the compound would involve little risk of

With his many years of experience in special military operations, Vice Admiral William H. McRaven (left) was a valuable source of advice in planning the attack on bin Laden's compound.

losing U.S. troops. Such a plan, however, would likely result in damage to the surrounding neighborhood and might injure or kill civilians living nearby. Digging a tunnel beneath the compound to allow the raid team to sneak in undetected was also considered. But experts determined that tunnels in the area were likely to flood with underground water. Sending a strike force of U.S. troops to attack the compound offered the greatest chance of ensuring that bin Laden was killed or captured. Unfortunately, it was also the least secretive way of approaching the compound.

Obama and his advisers discussed whether or not to inform the Pakistani government of a raid. The Americans had been warned not to conduct unauthorized military operations on Pakistani soil. Informing the Pakistanis of the mission, however, carried a huge risk that the compound's occupants would receive a warning and would escape before the raid. Obama's team ultimately decided that taking down bin Laden would be worth the possibility of damaging the United States' relationship with Pakistan.

By the conclusion of the meeting, it was decided that the two best options were to send a strike force into

President Obama knew that launching a raid on the Abbottabad compound could ruin relationships with President Asif Ali Zardari (left) and other Pakistani leaders.

the compound or to drop bombs from above. Both options would require a great deal of planning and practice.

Settling on a Plan

About two weeks later, details of both plans were presented to President Obama. Panetta and McRaven had developed a plan for using helicopters to send a team of Navy SEALs into the compound. Other top advisers still believed that bombing the compound was a safer choice. The two sides each argued their points to the president.

Although dropping bombs would avoid the loss of U.S.

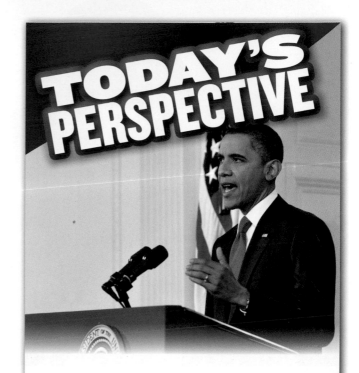

TODAY'S PERSPECTIVE

President Obama's decision on how to capture bin Laden was very difficult. Many advisers argued that bombing the compound would avoid the risk of U.S. soldiers being captured or killed. Obama, however, did not want a situation in which bin Laden was killed but his body could not be found. Without a body, no one could be certain that bin Laden was actually dead. People might accuse the U.S. government of lying about its success. As a result, Obama favored the plan in which Navy SEALs attacked the compound from the ground. Had the mission gone wrong, people would likely have blamed President Obama for making a deadly, irresponsible choice. The results, however, proved that he made the right choice.

SEALs go through intense training programs to prepare for the difficult missions they face.

soldiers, such an air strike would also destroy any useful evidence of al-Qaeda's activities in the compound. Perhaps most important, the bombing of the compound would destroy everything inside it—such as a dead body that would prove bin Laden had been killed.

A helicopter assault, however, would allow U.S. troops to enter the compound's buildings and come face-to-face with its occupants—and perhaps bin Laden himself. A ground assault would also allow the troops to search for computer files or documents containing information about al-Qaeda's terrorist activities. There was one possible problem with this plan. If the Pakistani government discovered the raid, it might send its own military forces in to attack the SEALs in the compound. Even though the risks were great, Obama and his advisers decided that sending in the SEALs was the best option for success.

Training the SEALs

McRaven chose 24 men and ordered them to travel to North Carolina for training. The SEALs were some of the best-trained soldiers in the entire U.S. military. Years of training and missions around the world had made them ready for almost anything. Even with the pressure of invading a foreign country and taking out the world's most famous terrorist, they would be able to keep their cool and perform their duties. When the team arrived in North Carolina on April 10, they were told about the compound and the mission. For the next five days, the SEALs practiced the mission using a replica of the compound that had been built deep in a thick forest.

They then traveled to a training area in the deserts of Nevada, where they practiced dropping out of helicopters on ropes. When they weren't training, the SEALs discussed strategy with McRaven and other leaders. They reviewed everything that could possibly go wrong with the mission—from the Pakistani government shooting down their helicopters to how they should deal with any civilians who got in the way of the raid.

As the SEALs trained, the details of the mission plan were finalized. The original plan called for two helicopters to carry the SEAL team from a U.S. base in Afghanistan to the compound in Abbottabad. A backup team would stay behind in Afghanistan. President Obama, however,

A FIRSTHAND LOOK AT

A SEAL'S EXPERIENCE

One of the SEALs who traveled to bin Laden's compound later wrote a book about his experiences. He also gave interviews to news reporters who wanted to hear the details of the raid. See page 60 for a link to watch an online video interview with the SEAL.

insisted that the backup forces travel into Pakistan as well, so they would be nearby in case of any emergency. Obama's decision turned out to be a wise change of plan.

The Final Decision

As the SEALs completed their training, the time to authorize the actual raid was rapidly approaching. On April 26, the SEALs began traveling from the United States to the U.S. base at Jalalabad, Afghanistan. Two days later, Obama met with Panetta and other top intelligence advisers to make a final decision. Panetta asked each person at the meeting how certain they were that bin Laden was in the compound. No one was 100 percent sure. Some were convinced of bin Laden's presence but lacked definite evidence. Others advised that the raid be postponed.

Those who were opposed to the raid said that the evidence merely indicated bin Laden was in the compound. They presented several alternate situations that could also be true. One possibility was that bin Laden had once lived at the compound but was no longer there. Another was that other top-ranking al-Qaeda leaders, not bin Laden, were using the house. The worst-case situation was that the compound might not have any connection to terrorists at all. Perhaps it was simply the home of a wealthy person who wanted privacy.

Obama carefully considered the arguments and determined that "at the end of the day, it's fifty-fifty" whether bin Laden was there or not. He ended the meeting and went home to think about the situation. The following day, President Obama made his final decision: the raid would proceed as planned. He knew there was a high risk of angering the Pakistani government or losing U.S. soldiers. But he was not willing to miss what might be the only chance the United States had to capture or kill its most-hated enemy.

Jalalabad, Afghanistan, a city with a population of around 170,000, is located near the border between Afghanistan and Pakistan.

CHAPTER 4

READY FOR ACTION

The White House Correspondents'
Association Dinner is an annual event
that is traditionally hosted by a popular
comedian and features a casual,
lighthearted speech from the president.

By Friday, April 29, the SEAL team was in place at Jalalabad and ready to begin its once-in-a-lifetime mission. Poor weather conditions, however, caused the raid to be delayed until Sunday, May 1. On Saturday morning, Obama phoned Jalalabad and spoke to McRaven about the mission. "Godspeed to you and your forces," he said. "Please pass on to them my personal thanks for their service and the message that I personally will be following this mission very closely." That evening, the president spoke to a gathering of journalists at the White House Correspondents' Association Dinner. He made jokes and seemed relaxed and at ease. No one there could have guessed the huge responsibility he now carried for having authorized one of the most daring raids in U.S. military history.

Before becoming secretary of state in 2009, Hillary Clinton was the country's first lady from 1993 until 2001 and a U.S. senator from 2001 to 2009.

Night Flight

On Sunday afternoon, Obama joined Vice President Joe Biden, Secretary of State Hillary Clinton, and other top-ranking U.S. leaders in the Situation Room of the White House. They were joined in a live video hookup with Panetta and McRaven. Panetta was at CIA headquarters in Langley, Virginia. McRaven was at the operation's base in Jalalabad. It was midafternoon in Washington, D.C., but late at night in Pakistan. Finally, after many weeks of careful planning and preparation, the raid was about to begin.

Two Black Hawk helicopters left the base at Jalalabad and flew toward Abbottabad. In addition to the SEAL team, also aboard the helicopters were two pilots, one crewman to take care of the copters, a translator, and a dog. The translator was a Pakistani-American who had never been on such a mission before. He was chosen for the raid because of his ability to speak one of Pakistan's languages, but he had no experience as a soldier. The dog, a Belgian shepherd named Cairo, was traveling with the SEALs to sniff out bombs and other traps that could have been rigged at the compound.

The U.S. Army has used UH 60 Black Hawk helicopters to transport troops and cargo since 1979.

Shortly after the Black Hawks began their journey, four Chinook helicopters took off from Jalalabad and headed into Pakistan. They would provide the backup that President Obama had demanded.

About 90 minutes after takeoff, the SEALs were above Abbottabad. Both Black Hawks and all four Chinooks had made it into Pakistan without alerting the local authorities. About 15,000 feet (4,572 m) above the ground, a stealth drone relayed live video of the Black Hawks' arrival to the president and his advisers back at the White House. They watched nervously as the two helicopters approached the compound.

As the first helicopter hovered above the compound, the pilot began struggling to keep it in the air. The air being pushed down by its blades was bouncing off the compound's high walls and back toward the copter. The helicopter began to fall. The SEALs would not be able to drop down from ropes as they had practiced. Instead, the pilot attempted to land the helicopter in the compound's yard. As he drew close to the ground, the helicopter's tail hit one of the compound's walls. A piece of the tail broke off and fell outside the compound as the rest of the helicopter thudded down inside. It was a rough landing, but everyone aboard was safe.

The second pilot was calm but cautious, as he watched the first helicopter land. He did not know if the other copter had been attacked or if it was just facing technical difficulty. To be safe, he chose to land in a field outside the compound.

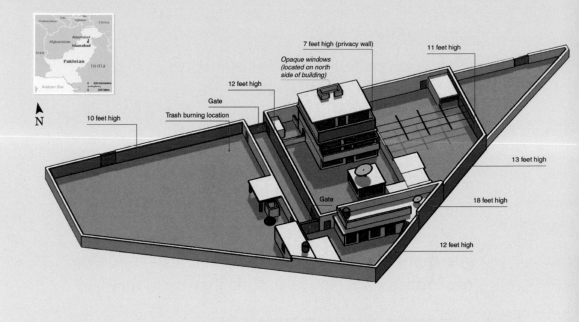

7 feet high (privacy wall)

11 feet high

Opaque windows
(located on north
side of building)

12 feet high

Gate

Trash burning location

10 feet high

N

13 feet high

Gate

18 feet high

12 feet high

The main house in bin Laden's compound was surrounded by high walls and a series of smaller buildings.

Geronimo

After sending a distress call to the backup Chinooks, the team began to recover from the raid's rocky start. The SEALs in the crashed copter were inside the compound's main wall, but they still needed to get through another wall to reach the main house. They placed explosives on the hinges of a gate and blew the door open. The SEALs in the second helicopter had an easier time entering the compound, as they discovered a door leading inside.

Four of the SEALs stayed behind with the dog to patrol the area and make certain that no one from the outside entered the compound. Meanwhile, the translator walked along the nearby street in case any civilians wandered by to check out the disturbance. His job was to pretend to be a Pakistani police officer and send away any curious civilians.

Inside the compound's walls, the SEALs formed into smaller groups and began making their way carefully toward the main building. They wore night-vision goggles to help them see and carried silenced rifles to muffle the noise their weapons made.

As one team approached the compound's guesthouse, they encountered Abu Ahmed al-Kuwaiti, the courier who had led U.S. intelligence to the

Night-vision goggles allow users to see in the dark, but do not offer the same sharp, colorful images that can be seen in well-lit environments.

compound. Al-Kuwaiti ran into the house to warn his wife and children of the attack. When he returned outside, he was carrying a gun. The SEALs quickly shot him and moved on. Al-Kuwaiti's brother Abrar, and Abrar's wife, were also killed as a group of SEALs approached the front door of the main house.

The SEAL groups joined together and entered the house. They moved through the building slowly and checked each room for threats. There was no one on the ground floor. On the second floor, bin Laden's son Khalid opened fire on the team. The SEALs killed him before Khalid was able to shoot anyone.

Official details regarding what happened next are a bit cloudy. One SEAL on the mission says that at this point, the team moved up the stairs to the third floor. The SEAL leading the group saw a face peering out from behind a bedroom door. He quickly fired several shots at the figure, not knowing if he had hit his target. The man disappeared into the dark room. The other members of the team burst into the room and saw the man on the ground. He had, in fact, been shot. It was then that the raiders realized they had gotten bin Laden. After avoiding his pursuers for almost a decade, Osama bin Laden had met his final fate at the hands of the U.S. military.

Another account claims that the SEALs knew it was bin Laden at the door. According to this version, the SEALs burst into the bedroom. Bin Laden stood behind two women. He was not holding a gun. One of the women began moving toward the SEALs. The SEAL in

A group of top U.S. officials monitored the raid on bin Laden's compound in real time, giving them a firsthand look as the SEALs successfully completed the mission of a lifetime.

front shot her in the leg to stop her. He was concerned that she and the other woman might be wearing explosive devices. To keep his teammates safe, the SEAL heroically tackled the two women to the ground and shielded the other SEALs with his body. Fortunately, the women were not wearing explosives. As the first SEAL tackled the women, another SEAL stepped up behind him, raised his rifle, and fired two shots at bin Laden. The terrorist was killed immediately.

What is known for certain is that after killing bin Laden, a SEAL then reported to McRaven over his radio, saying,

"Geronimo EKIA." *Geronimo* was the code word for "bin Laden." *EKIA* means "enemy killed in action." It was the message the world had been waiting to hear for 10 years.

McRaven immediately reported the good news to the people waiting anxiously at the White House. Calmly and quietly, Obama said aloud, "We got him."

The Way Out

The SEALs gathered up bin Laden's body, but the mission wasn't over yet. Four of the SEALs immediately began searching the compound for any potentially useful intelligence.

YESTERDAY'S HEADLINES

Bin Laden's death made headlines the day after the raid. Many newspapers reported the reactions of people around the world. According to the *New York Times*, "The news touched off an extraordinary outpouring of emotion as crowds gathered outside the White House, in Times Square and at the ground zero site, waving American flags, cheering, shouting, laughing and chanting, 'U.S.A., U.S.A.!'"

The *Wall Street Journal* reported the opinions of various world leaders. Israeli Prime Minister Benjamin Netanyahu called bin Laden's death "a resounding victory for justice," while British prime minister David Cameron referred to it as a "great relief."

A VIEW FROM ABROAD

As President Obama and his advisers had expected, Pakistani leaders were very displeased to learn about the raid on bin Laden's compound. The Pakistani government's biggest concern, however, was not that the United States had raided the compound without authorization. Instead, its leaders were embarrassed and angry that the U.S. forces had been able to slip in and out of their country without alerting Pakistani officials or its military. Despite this, Pakistani president Asif Ali Zardari offered his congratulations when President Obama telephoned him to explain what had happened.

They carried away computer equipment and documents. The others worked to round up the women and children who were living at the compound, and then restrained them to prevent any attacks as the SEALs were leaving. As the team was finishing up, a support Chinook arrived at the scene.

Before leaving, the SEALs used explosives to destroy the Black Hawk helicopter that had been damaged during landing. They wanted to make sure that no one would be able to repair it and use it. Then, only 38 minutes after first landing at the compound, they were back in the air again. Some SEALs rode in the Black Hawk, while others rode in the Chinook.

When they arrived back in Jalalabad, McRaven personally inspected bin Laden's body. He then ordered

Osama bin Laden's body was delivered to its final resting place in the Arabian Sea from the deck of a U.S. aircraft carrier.

it to be loaded onto an aircraft and flown to a U.S. carrier in the Arabian Sea, off the coast of Pakistan. There, the body was properly prepared for an Islamic burial, weighted down, and put into the sea.

A FIRSTHAND LOOK AT
PRESIDENT OBAMA'S ANNOUNCEMENT

Late at night back in the United States, President Obama made a special televised announcement to report that bin Laden was dead. See page 60 for a link to watch the announcement online.

MAP OF THE EVENTS

What Happened Where?

AFGHANISTAN

Kandahar, Afghanistan
Kandahar, Afghanistan, served as the home
base of the Taliban. On December 6, 2001,
the U.S. military and its allies took control of
the city, removing the Taliban from power.

Kandahar ●

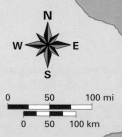

N
W E
S

0   50   100 mi
0   50   100 km

Arabian Sea

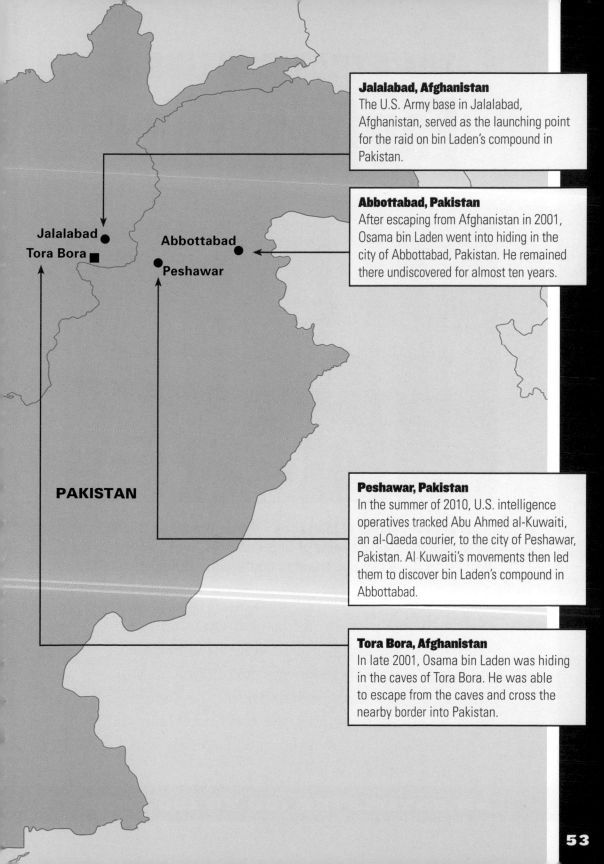

Jalalabad, Afghanistan
The U.S. Army base in Jalalabad, Afghanistan, served as the launching point for the raid on bin Laden's compound in Pakistan.

Abbottabad, Pakistan
After escaping from Afghanistan in 2001, Osama bin Laden went into hiding in the city of Abbottabad, Pakistan. He remained there undiscovered for almost ten years.

Jalalabad
Tora Bora
Abbottabad
Peshawar

Peshawar, Pakistan
In the summer of 2010, U.S. intelligence operatives tracked Abu Ahmed al-Kuwaiti, an al-Qaeda courier, to the city of Peshawar, Pakistan. Al-Kuwaiti's movements then led them to discover bin Laden's compound in Abbottabad.

PAKISTAN

Tora Bora, Afghanistan
In late 2001, Osama bin Laden was hiding in the caves of Tora Bora. He was able to escape from the caves and cross the nearby border into Pakistan.

Far from Over

In his announcement of bin Laden's death, President Obama recounted the tragic events of September 11, 2001, reminding the world why it was so important to capture bin Laden.

On May 1, 2011, at 11:35 p.m. eastern time, President Obama officially announced that Osama bin Laden had been killed. Huge crowds celebrated in front of the White House and in towns and cities across the country. As they did, Obama carefully explained how the U.S. intelligence community had traced bin Laden to Abbottabad. He called bin Laden's death "the most

AN ESTIMATED 100 TO 150 CORE

54

significant achievement to date in our nation's effort to defeat al-Qaeda." He also acknowledged, however, that the battle against terrorism was far from over. "There's no doubt that al-Qaeda will continue to pursue attacks against us," he said. "We must—and we will—remain vigilant at home and abroad."

On May 6, al-Qaeda issued a statement in which it promised to seek revenge for bin Laden's death. The same day, Obama, Vice President Biden, and others flew to Fort Campbell, Kentucky, where they personally thanked the members of the raid team for their heroic service. Although al-Qaeda was still operating, a major blow had been struck against terrorism. The United States was prepared to face the future with optimism.

For many who were affected by the attacks of September 11, 2001, bin Laden's death brought a sense of closure.

AL-QAEDA MEMBERS REMAIN IN PAKISTAN.

Leon Panetta

George W. Bush

Leon Panetta (1938–) was the director of the Central Intelligence Agency. Under his leadership, the CIA conducted surveillance of bin Laden's compound and provided the information necessary to conduct a raid.

George W. Bush (1946–) was the 43rd president of the United States. He began the hunt for Osama bin Laden shortly after the September 11 attacks.

William McRaven (1955–) was a commander of the U.S. Joint Special Operations Command. He led the planning and execution of the raid on bin Laden's compound.

Osama bin Laden (1957–2011) was the founder and leader of the Islamic terrorist group al-Qaeda. Under his leadership, al-Qaeda was responsible for the terrorist attacks against the United States on September 11, 2001.

Barack Obama (1961–) was the 44th president of the United States. During his administration, the nation intensified its search for Osama bin Laden.

Osama bin Laden

Abu Ahmed al-Kuwaiti (?–2011) was a courier for al-Qaeda. By following him, U.S. intelligence operatives were able to discover the location of Osama bin Laden's hiding place in Abbottabad, Pakistan.

Barack Obama

TIMELINE

1957

Osama bin Laden is born in Saudi Arabia.

1979

The Soviet Union invades Afghanistan; bin Laden begins working with Islamic militants to fight the Soviets.

2001

September 11
Al-Qaeda terrorists hijack four commercial jets and attack the United States.

October 7
The United States begins a war against the Taliban in Afghanistan.

December
Bin Laden escapes from Tora Bora and goes into hiding in Pakistan.

2008

Barack Obama wins the U.S. presidential election.

1988

Bin Laden builds a computer database of Islamic militants and uses it to form al-Qaeda.

1994

The Taliban forms and begins to seize control in Afghanistan.

2009

The search for bin Laden intensifies under Obama's command.

2010

Bin Laden's compound is discovered in Abbottabad, Pakistan.

2011

May 1
A team of U.S. Navy SEALs successfully raids Osama bin Laden's compound and kills him.

LIVING HISTORY

Primary sources provide firsthand evidence about a topic. Witnesses to a historical event create primary sources. They include autobiographies, newspaper reports of the time, oral histories, photographs, and memoirs. A secondary source analyzes primary sources and is one step or more removed from the event. Secondary sources include textbooks, encyclopedias, and commentaries. To view the following primary and secondary sources, go to www.factsfornow.scholastic.com. Enter the keywords **Hunt for Bin Laden** and look for the Living History logo Σ¦.

Σ¦ **Bin Laden's Post-9/11 Video** Shortly after September 11, Osama bin Laden released a video in which he acknowledged al-Qaeda's responsibility for the attacks. He also promised that he was planning further attacks against the United States.

Σ¦ **President Obama's Announcement** Millions of people around the world watched as President Obama announced that a team of Navy SEALs had killed Osama bin Laden.

Σ¦ **A SEAL's Experience** Matt Bissonnette, a member of the SEAL team that raided bin Laden's compound, wrote a book and discussed his experiences with the media. Watch a video of Bissonnette, using the name Mark Owen, as he discusses the details of the raid with Scott Pelley of CBS News.

Σ¦ **The 2008 Presidential Debates** During the 2008 presidential debates, Barack Obama stated that he would do whatever it took to stop bin Laden. Watch a video of a debate to see Obama discuss what he would do if bin Laden were discovered in Pakistan.

RESOURCES

Books

Benoit, Peter. *September 11: We Will Never Forget*. New York: Children's Press, 2012.

Lunis, Natalie. *The Takedown of Osama bin Laden*. New York: Bearport Publishing, 2012.

Zeiger, Jennifer. *The War in Afghanistan*. New York: Children's Press, 2012.

Visit this Scholastic Web site for more information on the hunt for bin Laden:
www.factsfornow.scholastic.com
Enter the keywords Hunt for Bin Laden

GLOSSARY

civilians (suh-VIL-yuhnz) people who are not members of the armed forces or a police force

couriers (KUR-ee-urz) people who carry messages or packages for somebody else

drones (DROHNZ) military aircraft without a pilot that are controlled remotely

extremist (ik-STREE-mist) believing in or resorting to measures beyond the norm, especially in politics

hijacked (HYE-jakt) having taken illegal control of a vehicle and forced its pilot or driver to go somewhere

intelligence (in-TEL-uh-junhts) secret information about an enemy

operatives (AH-pur-uh-tivz) secret agents or spies

raids (RAYDZ) sudden, surprise attacks on places

safe house (SAYF HOUS) a house in a secret location, used by spies

sovereignty (SAHV-ruhn-tee) the authority of a state to govern itself or another state

stealth (STELTH) marked by or acting with quiet, caution, and secrecy meant to avoid notice

surveillance (sur-VAY-luhns) close observation of a person or group

terrain (tuh-RAYN) an area of land

Page numbers in *italics* indicate illustrations.

ABOUT THE AUTHOR

Josh Gregory writes and edits books for kids. He lives in Chicago, Illinois.